IN THE FOREST

IN THE FOREST

A PORTFOLIO OF PAINTINGS

JIM ARNOSKY

LOTHROP, LEE & SHEPARD BOOKS / NEW YORK

First Edition
1 2 3 4 5 6 7 8 9 10

Library of Congress Cataloging in Publication Data
Arnosky, Jim. In the forest : a portfolio of paintings / by Jim Arnosky.
p   cm.   Summary: The noted artist presents oil paintings depicting the forest at different
times of the day during the fall and winter and discusses the plants and animals that live there.
ISBN 0-688-08162-2. — ISBN 0-688-09138-5 (lib. bdg.)
1. Forest ecology—Pictorial works—Juvenile literature. [1. Forest ecology—Pictorial works.
2. Ecology—Pictorial works.]
I. Title.   QH541.5.F6A76   1989   759.13—dc19
89-2341   CIP   AC

This book is dedicated to
Guy Labounty

INTRODUCTION

The forest I know is always changing, growing. It is a forest where grassy fields revert to brush and then to seedling trees. It is a single slender stem spiraling taller, a supple twig reaching toward a shaft of light. It is a forest stored down in the roots of sawed-off stumps kept vital by soil and seeping water—tomorrow's trees, urged ever upward by the sun. My forest is a place of hidden springs and tumbling streams, and it is inhabited by animals that are shy and always hiding.

This book is a little bit of forest you can hold, composed of paintings done outdoors, printed on paper made from forest trees, and bound together by two seasons.

Jim Arnosky
Ramtails 1989

HILLSIDE—MIXED WOODS

There had just been two whole days of rain. Finally the overcast sky was beginning to clear. Shafts of sunlight streamed through holes in the clouds and brightened long strips of the soggy ground. The air was cool and moving and scented with the fragrance of bark. Chickadees were making funny tweezling sounds, calling to one another amid the sheltering boughs of hemlocks. I painted the hillside scene while standing under the shelter of an umbrella. In the woods, raindrops were still falling, dripping from high branches.

The row of granite boulders in the center of the scene, remains of an old stone wall, shows that the wooded hill was once open farmland. When settlers first came to this place, they found a hilly, rugged, rocky land covered with virgin timber. To clear the land for farming, they had to fell the giant trees and burn the stumps. They dug out the boulders, dragged them off, and piled them neatly, making long walls that would later serve as fences separating pastures from meadows from woodlots. The walls also formed the boundaries of individual farms.

Imagine this scene without the trees—a grassy slope all the way up to the hilltop horizon. Picture the boulders as the foundation of a complete and sturdy wall dividing the hill in halves. That is the way this hillside looked a hundred years ago.

As soon as the farming here ceased, the forest began its comeback. The grass gave way to weeds and brush. Then seedling trees—first pioneer poplars and evergreens, later birches, maples, oaks, and hornbeams—took hold. This healthy mix of trees is still growing. In time, the maturing maples and oaks will compete to dominate the woods, and the hillside once again will change.

FIR STAND

In the mixed woods, sunlight shines down through gaps between trees of various sizes and shapes. In this stand of balsam firs, the treetops are uniform in height and similarly shaped. The balsams' evergreen branches overlap and form a tightly closed canopy, which very little light can penetrate. The only things growing on the forest floor are shade-loving mosses, ferns, and more fir trees. The young firs absorb whatever sunlight angles down to them between the tall tree trunks.

The surface of the soil under the firs is dry and porous. You sink an inch with every step, but the soles of your boots remain clean. It makes you wonder what supports the tall, topheavy firs. The answer lies beneath. The land below is moist, almost swampy, with many large boulders—plenty of rock and muck for the spreading roots of evergreens to hold on to. I am told that somewhere in this fir forest, covered by moss and roots, is an old-time deep well, lined with boulders and brimming with ice-cold spring water. I've searched, but cannot find it. I have found a small brook, though, that meanders all through the woods. The brook runs mostly out of sight, in a gully. The stream would go unnoticed if it wasn't for the gurgling sound it makes as it flows on its pebbled bed. At one point the brook forks, forming two rivulets, one of which runs down under the ground. Water is kept secret in this place.

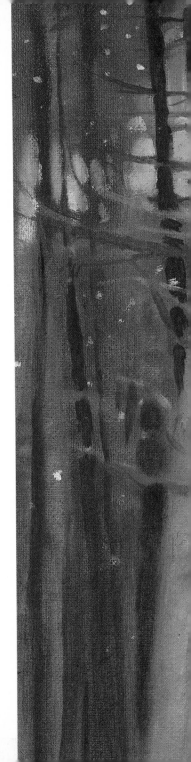

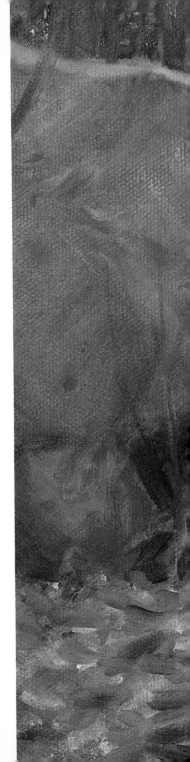

BROOK

At the edge of the firs, the rivulet resurfaces and soon rejoins the other fork. From there the brook runs strong and full, winding its way between and around large, moss-covered boulders, digging and running under the roots of trees, and falling over steps of granite ledge. Its twisting, tumbling course causes the water to swirl as it flows, forming tiny surface whirlpools that cast small circular shadows, each with a bright halo of magnified light, on the stream's sandy bed.

At this place the brook is surrounded by birch, maple, and hemlock trees. One hemlock stands beside the pool, leaning over the stream as trees near water do. The scene here is of the brook at midday, when sunlight shines directly down and illuminates the sandy bottom, giving the water a warm amber glow. There is a light dusting of snow on the leafy ground.

I visit this spot throughout the year, most frequently in spring and fall. In spring I look for fiddlehead ferns unfurling and for wake-robin and trout lily, the first wild flowers that bloom in the dappled sunlight on the stream banks. In fall I come to watch the brook's tiny trout spawn. The trout are native brookies with black backs and flashing amber sides. It is wonderful to see them making their way upstream to their spawning pools, leaping up and over each small falls they come to. Sometimes a trout will disappear under boulders in the head of a lower pool and seconds later emerge, presumably by some hidden stony stairway, into the pool above.

COPSE

Along the brook there is an open spot, a copse, where grasses, briars, brush, and vines grow—a haven for rabbits, mice, squirrels, and birds. Here the brook flows slowly in a shallow channel that wends its way through the tangle. You cannot see the brook from this point. It is beyond the sunlit brush. Water diverted from the main stream by the thickly matted vegetation seeps into the soil, making the ground marshy all through the copse. Alder trees, whose crooked stems and branches grow well in marshy soil, are growing here.

This place once was a shady spot dominated by a large ash tree. The tree was twenty inches in diameter and sixty feet tall. When its branches began to interfere with a power line that spans the area, the power company sent a crew to saw the tree down. With the ash gone, the younger trees around shot upward in the sunny gap, each one racing to be the next to touch the high wire.

On the morning I decided to paint the copse, I had been simply passing by it on my way to the brook. Suddenly a grouse exploded noisily from the brush, flying straight upward with rapid wing beats. Then, with wings outstretched, the bird sailed away over the tan and gold dry grasses of the adjacent field. The grouse drew my attention to the copse as a unique forest place. I painted the scene and hid the grouse in it. If you can't find the bird in the painting, I'll understand. I never would have noticed it myself if it hadn't flown.

CLEARING

It was late in the afternoon when I came upon the deer, a doe, in a forest clearing created by the falling of a number of large hemlock trees. The deer was lying down, resting on some dry grasses. She saw me but, mysteriously, showed no fear. On a blank canvas I sketched the deer once as she lay, again as she slowly stood and stretched, and once more while she moved away, stepping carefully over the branches and trunk of a fallen tree. I watched as she picked her way all through the cluttered clearing and disappeared in the hemlock woods. Just then I heard a loud cracking noise behind me and spun around to see the top half of another hemlock, a huge and rotted tree, come crashing to the ground. There was no wind. The tree was simply ripe to break and fall.

The next day I returned and painted the clearing scene on the same canvas, around my life sketch of the deer at rest. As I worked I saw the doe again. This time she was more wary. She stayed in the forest, moving slowly and silently between the tree trunks, all the while staring out at me. I continued painting, keeping one eye on my canvas and the other on the watching deer.

SOFTWOODS

There is a kind of magic in the forest—in the moment a tree falls without the push of wind, or in the way a footprint pressed into moss quickly disappears. And it is magical to see a hazy shaft of sun coming through the treetops, brightly lighting the needles of a tiny evergreen.

This place, which sunlight visits briefly and only once a day, has cast its spell on me. It is here that a year or so ago I saw my only lynx. The lynx had just come out of an adjacent bog and was about to enter the hemlock wood when we saw each other. For long seconds we stood staring into each other's eyes. I was entranced and could not move. The lynx took a step, and then another, and slowly padded into the hemlocks out of sight.

Along with hemlock trees there are spruce trees growing here and some tamaracks spreading spottily from the bog. This place filled with coniferous trees is called a softwood forest because conifers (evergreens) are considered to have softer, pulpier wood than deciduous (broadleaf) trees. Deciduous trees are called hardwoods. I painted this softwoods scene on a December morning during the short time the light was in the forest. It was quite cold that morning, but the sunlight streaming down through the trees made the place look warm.

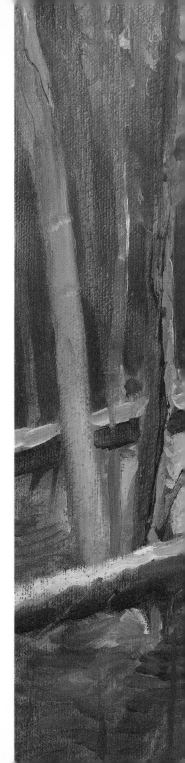

BEAVER POND

The beaver pond rests neatly in a cup-shaped hollow less than seventy-five feet across. The forest trees on one side of the pond are mostly softwoods. Those growing on the other side are hardwoods. Beavers prefer hardwood trees as food and to use as building material. The hardwoods are kept thinned out by the beavers' constant felling of trees. The softwood trees have grown thick and tall, ignored for many years by the beavers living here. The pond is fed by an ice-cold brook that tumbles downhill over large granite boulders. The surface of the pond is frozen now, except where the brook flows in and along the top of the dam where the overflow spills out.

The beavers are inside the lodge, and chances are they won't come out in the open again until spring. When hungry, a beaver swims out of the lodge to a winter store of food—a submerged pile of twigs and branches. Taking a twig or two from the pile, the beaver returns to the lodge to eat. Once, while walking on the frozen surface of another beaver pond, I heard a scratching sound. Looking down, I saw the body of a beaver swimming under the ice. The beaver was carrying a long food stick, and the stick, dragging against the under surface of the ice, caused the scratching noise.

The only sound I heard while painting this beaver pond was that of water trickling musically over the dam. During a break, I took a walk around the hollow and up the icy brook. All along the book, and in the woods around, were tiny chewed-off stumps of trees the beavers had felled.

LOGGING ROAD

Wherever loggers—beaver or human—work, they create a network of trails as they get to and drag out the timber they cut down. Beaver trails emanate from the beaver pond outward, but not too far into the surrounding woods. The logging trails that people make are really rustic roads. They may stretch out for miles, leading down into hollows, up over ridges, anywhere the trees have grown mature enough to cut.

Large animals such as moose, bear, and deer use logging roads, often sticking right to them as they travel through the cut-down areas, feeding on the brushy plants that thrive in open places. Smaller animals connect the logging roads with pathways of their own, called game trails, that wind all through the surrounding thickets.

When I'm feeling my wildest and wish to be someplace rugged and remote, I come here. This place was logged about five years ago. The trees were all mature maples. I hated to see the old maples go, but for every maple tree the loggers took, thousands more have grown. The scene I've painted here is not the old forest or a new forest, but the forest continuing.

While I was adding the final brush strokes to this canvas, a deep-voiced animal—a coyote, I think—began growling at me from behind a dense screen of maple saplings. The animal never showed itself, but kept up its steady growling. The sound made me feel unsafe, yet I was not frightened. Then, just as suddenly as it began, the growling stopped.

GAME TRAIL—SUNSET

One evening, while I was on my way out of the forest, the sunset was so spectacular that I quickly set up my easel and canvas and rapidly painted all the colors I was seeing. The sunset lasted only five minutes longer. Then the sky turned uniformly dark blue.

As I was packing up to leave, I noticed a line of fox tracks on a game trail that wound down around the trees and brush covering the sloping land. The footprints looked fresh, and I wondered if the fox had walked down the trail sometime during the sunset—perhaps only moments before I came upon the scene.

The next evening I returned to the same spot. On the canvas on which I had painted the colorful sunset, I began to add the darkening landscape. I painted the tree-lined horizon first, and then, lower on the canvas, I painted the fox as I imagined it might have looked walking down the slope. It was twilight when I painted the foreground, adding only objects I could see clearly. At nightfall I still could make out some details of trees and brush. The human eye adjusts amazingly well to darkness as long as you do not turn on any artificial light, even for an instant. A flash of bright light ruins night vision.

I painted well into the night, adding browns, maroons, greens, and blacks to match the dark blur of nighttime color. An animal stirred in the brush behind me and moved on. I could hear its soft footfalls. Perhaps it was the fox!

GREAT WHITE PINE

In the forest every tree is a living place, anchored in earth and towering upward to the sky. In old age a tree becomes a monument to sun, water, and time. I had been thinking of a tree I had once found—a huge and regal tree that, though it may not be the oldest, is certainly the largest tree I have ever seen. I thought this tree was somewhere far away, high on a ridge, and that it was a giant oak or maple. Then the other day some impulse made me look for it in the forest very near my home. I walked as if I was being guided through the snowy woods, down a hollow directly to this venerable white pine—the tree of my memory. It was not a far-off oak or maple after all.

I stood below the great tree. Its trunk, twelve feet in circumference at the base, stands nearly one hundred feet tall. Its massive limbs—each one like a separate tree—grow vertically, reaching heights of one hundred ten to one hundred twenty-five feet. It was a windy day, and when the limbs swayed in the air the wood inside them moaned and cracked from the strain.

This tree has lived longer than two centuries. It is the parent tree of nearly every white pine in the vicinity. Considering that less than one hundred years ago the surrounding countryside was mostly open farmland, this enduring pine is older than the whole forest.

WINTER HARDWOODS

It is midwinter, and everywhere the forest is transformed by ice and snow. The clearing has become a whitened field, lumpy with the buried forms of fallen trees. In the copse the tangled brush is flattened under heavy snow. Rabbits, mice, and grouse that once could hide amid the airy vegetation must now make holes and tunnels in the white stuff. The brook is frozen over and blanketed with snowflakes. The softwood forest is a wonderland of passageways in, around, and under snow-laden boughs. Hardwood tree trunks look like crooked sticks silhouetted against the snow. Look long at the hardwoods on a snowy hillside and you begin to separate the silhouettes by color. Maple trunks are brown. Poplars are pale gray. Beech trees have a bluish tint. And birches, depending on their species, can be pink, white, maroon, bronze, and even gold.

In winter, a hardwood forest is an open, highly visible place. You can look between the tree trunks and spot a boulder on the ground an acre away. Any contour in the land stands out, so that even a casual passerby can get a sense of where the terrain is gently sloped, terraced, or angled steeply upward. On a clear day, slowly scan a winter hardwoods and you may see a pileated woodpecker flying from tree to tree or a red fox traversing the snow.

On this snowy day, as I painted the hardwood scene, I neither saw nor heard any animals or birds. Every forest creature had taken shelter from the storm. The only footprints were my own, and those were quickly blotted out by falling snow.

Paintings executed in oils on canvas. Oil paints were the medium of choice because the pictures were painted outdoors in cold weather, and oils do not freeze. To economize on weight carried while hiking, Mr. Arnosky limited his palette to six colors: red, light yellow, yellow ochre, permanent blue, raw umber, and white.

Designed by Jim Arnosky.
Typography and layout by Cindy Simon. Composed by Expertype, Inc. in 11 pt. Schneidler Medium.

Color separations by Accent on Color.
Printed on Sterling Litho Satin Matte paper by General Offset Company, Inc.